Simply Soul
Vegetarian Soup Recipes

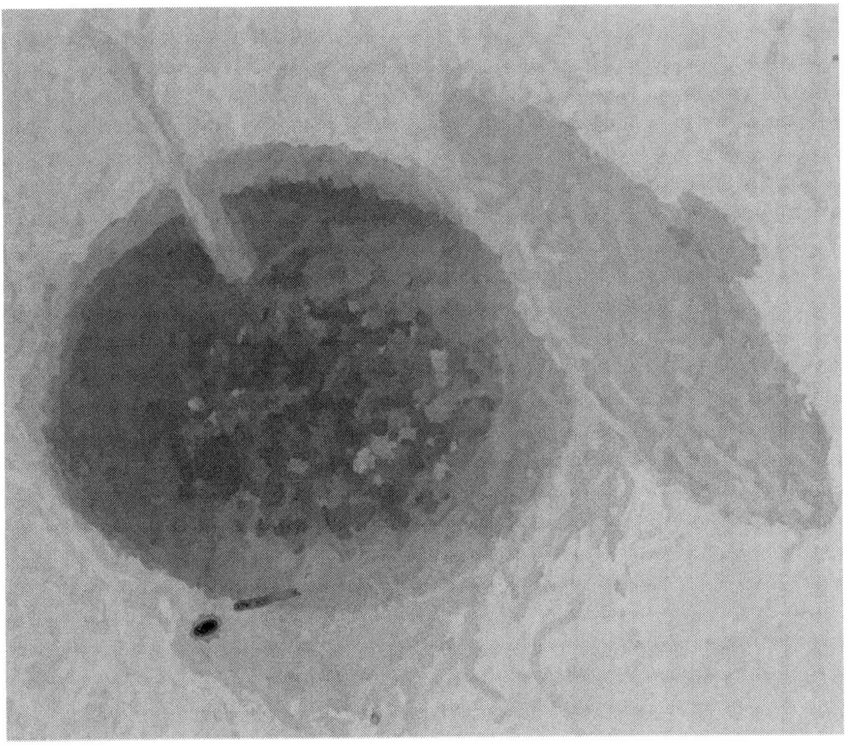

By Vanessa Cross

Table of Content

Herb Broth for Summer Soups	1
Vegetable Broth	2
Classic Vegetable Soup	3
Sis's Vegetable Soup	4
Vegetable Barley Soup	5
Clear Japanese Soup	5
French Onion Soup	6
Onion Soup Fondue	7
Potato Soup	8
Cream of Spinach	9
Senegalese Soup	10-11
Tomato Soup	12
Tomato-Basil Bisque	13
Vegetable Soup with Basil Pesto	14
Caribbean Tomato & Peanut Soup	15
Caribbean Papaya & Garlic Soup	16
Cuban Vegetarian Black Bean Soup	17
Bean Soup	18
Lentil Soup	19
Green Summer Soup	20
Carrot Cream Soup	21
Avocado & Ginger Vichyssoise	22
Veggie Chili	23
Lima Bean Soup	24
Hawaiian Red Bean Soup	25

Sweet Potato Soup	26
Chilled Beetroot Soup	27
Fresh Summer Salad in a Soup	28
Perky Squash Soup	29
Collar Green Pistou	30
Turnip Green Soup	31
Cold Cucumber Soup	32
Smokey Red Pepper Soup	33
Creamy Tofu Tomato Soup	34
Onion Soup	35
Cabbage Soup	36
Cream of Broccoli Soup	37
Hot and Sour Soup	38
Indian Pea Soup	39
Potato and Leek Soup	40
Zucchini and Potato Cream Soup	41
Vegetable Gumbo	42
Chilled Fruit Soup	43
L.A.'s Minted Berry Soup	44

Simply Soul

Vegetarian Soup Recipes

© Vanessa Cross, 2017

Introduction

There is a general movement by people to take control of their health by taking control of their nutrition. This book is designed to help you to prepare delicious and quick vegetarian soups. Soups can become a nutritional and economical part of your meal plans. They are also an excellent option for vegetarians who want to diversify their menus. In fact, the types of vegetables that can be used in soups are endless and can be supplemented with beans, roots, mushrooms and even fruits. We hope that some of the dozens of simple and tasty recipes here become favorites for you, your family and friends.

Pairings

Soups love to be paired with salads and sandwiches. If a soup is paired with another main dish or as an appetizer, the proper serving is about one cup. When the soup is the main course, the serving size may be as much as two cups. Add fresh bread to any of the recipes in this soup cook-book to make a hearty meal.

Timing

As a general tip, keep watch on a soup's cooking time. Vegetable based soups are quick cookers. Cook strong-juiced vegetables, such as hearty greens, until they are tender but not over cooked. Prolonged cooking of vegetables can produce an unpleasant smell from sulphur compounds emitted from a covered kettle. An open pan covered in sufficient water eliminates this problem.

Storing

You can make large batches of a soup and store it in individual containers in your freezer for at least two months. To prepare left-over soups for freezing, divide the soup into quantities that will be useful later. Store soups in containers that can serve as individual meal portions or family portions. To keep refrigerated soups from spoiling, reheat them to the boiling point every third day.

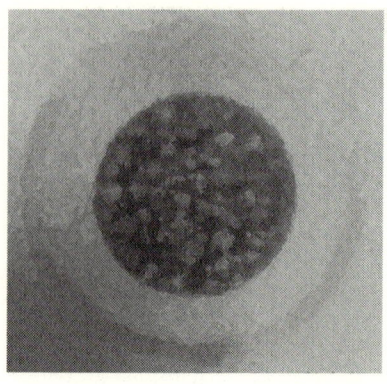

A vegetable broth is the liquid in which vegetables have been cooked. Broth contains a vegetable's flavors, minerals and vitamins. For a highly flavorful broth, add vegetables such as cabbage or turnips to your broth boil. To avoid bitterness, do not cook your vegetable broths for more than 30 minutes. Vegetable broth can be used to replace any recipe that calls for chicken or meat stock.

Herb Broth for Summer Soups

1 cup of herbs (e.g., parsley, celery, mint, basil, chives, lucerne, or a combination)
4-8 cups of boiling water
1 onion, chopped
2 vegetable bouillon cubes
Salt to taste

Pour boiling water over herbs and chopped onion. Stand, then add the crumbled bouillon cubes and a little salt. Strain and store in containers that are good for your meal proportion requirements. The stock can be used as a base for making a healthy, quick soup.

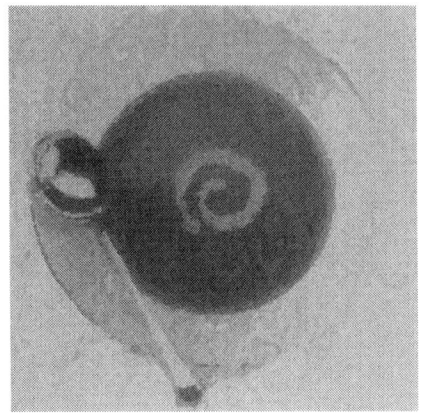

Vegetable Broth

2 leeks, sliced thin
2 stalks celery with leaves, sliced and chopped
2 onions, sliced or chopped
4 carrots, chopped
4 sprigs parsley with stems, chopped
1 teaspoon dried thyme
1 bay leaf
¼ teaspoon salt
6 cups of water

For this vegetable broth, place all the ingredients into a large soup pot. Bring slowly to a boil, then reduce the heat and simmer very gently for about 30 minutes, skimming off any vegetable fat that rises to the surface. Strain and cool uncovered. This vegetable broth can be stored in refrigerator containers for future use in many of the vegetable soup recipe variations in this book.

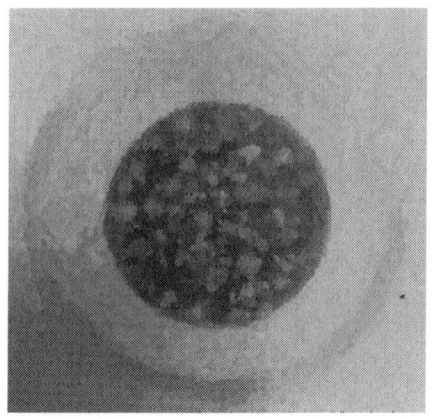

Classic Vegetable Soup

4 tablespoons carrots, diced
2 celery stalks with leaves, diced
½ onion, chopped
1 small turnip, peeled and diced
1 medium potato, peeled and diced
5 cups vegetable broth
1 tablespoon buttermilk
1 tablespoon finely chopped parsley
Salt to taste
Freshly ground pepper to taste

Melt the butter in a soup pot, then add the carrots, celery, onion, turnip and potato. Cook over low heat, stirring, for about 10 minutes. This soup is easily turned into a vegetable stew by adding items like tomatoes, shredded cabbage, green beans and corn. After cooking the vegetables in butter, add the broth, partially cover, and simmer for about 30 minutes or until the vegetables are tender.

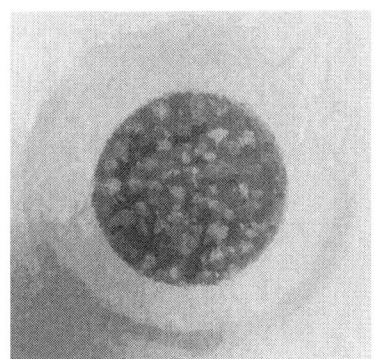

Sis's Vegetable Soup

2 medium Irish potatoes, cubed
2 medium carrots, sliced thin
1 onion, chopped
1 bell pepper, chopped
2 vegetable cubes
1 (16 oz.) pkg. frozen mixed vegetable soup mix with tomatoes
1 fresh tomato (or tomato sauce)
2 tbsp. cooking oil
Salt, red pepper, and black pepper to taste
2 qt. water

Prepare vegetables and add all other ingredients. Cook slowly until vegetables are tender, adding more water if necessary. You may add ¼ cup raw rice if you like thicker soup. Note: cubes are salty so dissolve in water and taste before adding salt to soup.

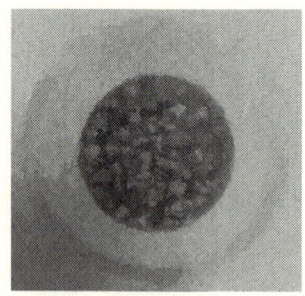

Vegetable Barley Soup

1 cup barley
6 cups of water
½ cup parsley, chopped
2 cups frozen mixed vegetables
1 onion, chopped
Pepper and salt to taste

Cook all the ingredients in a large pot over medium heat until barley is tender. Makes 6-8 servings.

Clear Japanese Soup

1 ½ qt. vegetable broth
1/3 cup dry sherry
4 ½ tsp. soy sauce
1 lemon, thinly sliced

Garnishes:
5 to 6 fresh mushrooms, sliced
2 green onions and tops, sliced diagonally
1 carrot, very thinly sliced.

Bring the broth to simmer in large saucepan. Add sherry and soy sauce. Simmer 2 to 3 minutes. Ladle soup into small bowls; float a lemon slice in each bowl. Arrange garnishes on tray and add to soup as desired. Serves 6.

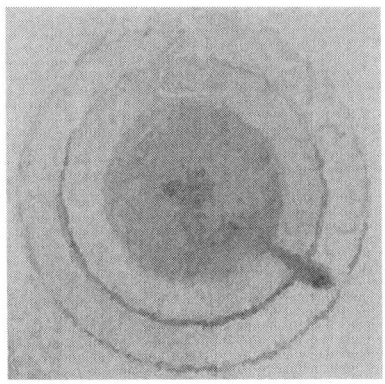

French Onion Soup

2 cups sliced onions
2 tablespoons buttermilk
1-1/2 quarts boiling water
1 cup diced celery
Salt to taste
5 slices of bread
Grated parmesan cheese

Sautée onions in butter until lightly browned. Add browned onions and celery and simmer until tender, about 1 hour. Toast bread, trim off crusts, cut in strips and float on top of bowlfuls of soup. Sprinkle grated cheese generously over top strips. Quick roast broil to top layer.

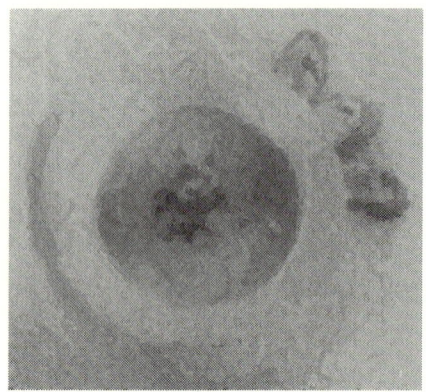

Onion Soup Fondue

¾ cup unsalted butter
4 to 6 large onions, thinly sliced
8 cups of vegetable broth
White pepper
12 ounces Monterey Jack cheese
French or sourdough bread, sliced 1 inch thick
Garlic Toast

Melt butter in large kettle, add onions, and sauté until transparent, but not browned. Add vegetable broth. Cover and simmer 2 to 3 hours. Remove from heat and refrigerate overnight or several hours. Reheat and season to taste with white pepper. Slice cheese into 12 slices. Lightly toast 12 bread slices and top each with 1 slice Jack cheese. Pour soup into individually ovenproof serving bowls and top with slice of bread and cheese. Run bowls under broiler just until the cheese bubbles and is soft but not browned. Serve with Garlic Toast on the side.

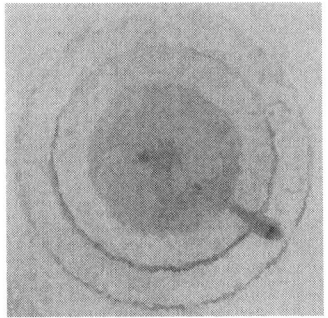

Potato Soup

2 medium-sliced potatoes, cubed
2 medium-sized onions, chopped
5 carrots, peeled and sliced
½ teaspoon salt
¼ tsp. paprika
2 tablespoons butter
2 cups of vegetable stock

Cook potatoes, chopped onions and carrots in the vegetable stock until tender. Put mixture through a potato masher ricer or place in a liquefier. Beat in butter and thin soup to desired consistency with additional stock. Sprinkle with salt and paprika. Garnish with chopped parsley before serving. Makes 4 cups.

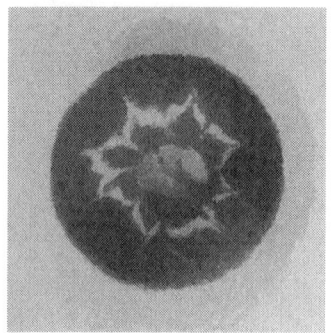

Cream of Spinach

2 pounds of spinach
2 tablespoons apricot-kernel oil
4 cups waters
4 teaspoons vegetable broth
1 tablespoon grated onion
Vegetable salt
Paprika

Wash spinach well. While moist place in covered saucepan and cook for six minutes. Put through a strainer. Preheat oil in skillet and sauté grated onions for five minutes over low heat. Stir in gradually 4 cups of vegetable broth, simmer slowly for five minutes. Season with salt and paprika, add spinach and heat well. Serve with wheat croutons. Makes 5 cups.

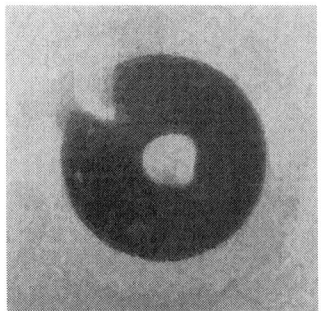

Senegalese Soup

2 tablespoons buttermilk
1 small onion, chopped
1 carrot, chopped
1 celery stalk, chopped
1 teaspoon curry powder
3 sticks cinnamon
1 tsp. whole cloves
2 bay leaves
1 tablespoon red currant jelly
1 tablespoon tomato puree
2-1/4 tablespoon. Tomato puree
2-1/4 tablespoons almond paste
5 cups vegetable broth
3 tablespoons buttermilk
3 tablespoons flour
2 cups heavy cream
Coconut, grated and toasted

In a large pan, melt 2 tablespoons of butter. Cook the onion, carrot, and celery in the butter over moderate heat, stirring, until they are tender (about 8-10 minutes). Add the curry powder and blend thoroughly with the vegetables. Add and mix in the cinnamon, cloves, bay leaves, jelly, tomato puree, almond paste, and vegetable broth. Bring to a boil and simmer for 1 hour, skimming off the foam that rises to the surface.

Kneed 3 tablespoons of butter with 3 tablespoons of flour.

Gradually blend small pieces of this paste into the soup, using a wire whisk. Cook until slightly thickened (5-6 minutes). Strain and taste for seasonings; add salt and pepper to taste. Cool and refrigerate for at least three hours. Just before leaving on your picnic, add well-chilled cream and combine thoroughly with the soup. Carry the toasted coconut in a separate container. Garnish each serving with a generous sprinkle of coconut. Serves 6-8.

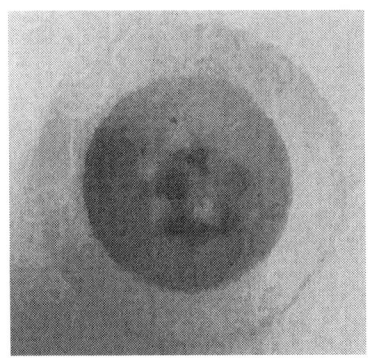

Tomato Soup

2 pounds and 8 ounces of tomatoes
1 ounce of butter
1 bay leaf
1 heaped teaspoon basil
½ teaspoon thyme
½ pint vegetable stock
¼ pint of milk
1-2 teaspoons sugar
Salt to taste
Pepper to taste

Scald the tomatoes and peel and slice them. Melt the butter and sauté the tomatoes with herbs. Cover and cook for about 30 minutes. Liquidize and if necessary put through a sieve. Return to pan and add the stock. Bring up to simmering point and turn heat down. Stir in the milk. Heat through but do not boil. Season with sugar, salt and pepper to taste.

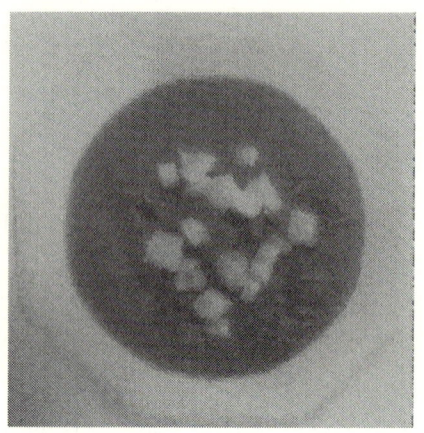

Tomato-Basil Bisque

3 cups of tomato soup
1 (14-1/4-oz.) can diced fire-roasted tomatoes
2-1/2 cups buttermilk
2 tbsp. chopped fresh basil
1/4-tsp. freshly ground black pepper

Cook ingredients in a 3-saucepan over medium heat, stirring often, 6 to 8 minutes or until thoroughly heated. Serve immediately with desired toppings. Makes about 7 cups.

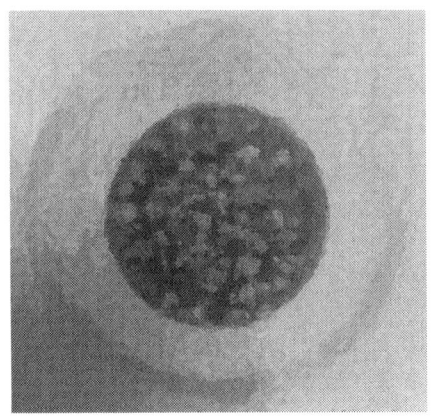

Vegetable Soup with Basil Pesto

2 medium carrots, chopped
2 celery ribs, chopped
1 large sweet onion, chopped
4 garlic cloves, minced
1 tsp. minced fresh thyme
1 tbsp. olive oil
2 (32-oz.) containers organic vegetable broth
2 plum tomatoes, seeded and chopped
1 medium zucchini, chopped
1-1/4 tsp. kosher salt
½ tsp. freshly ground black pepper
1 (15-oz.) can cannellini beans, drained and rinsed
½ cup uncooked mini farfalle (bow-tie) pasta
Basil pesto

Sauté carrots and next 4 ingredients in hot oil in a Dutch oven over medium-high heat 8 to 10 minutes or until vegetables are tender. Stir in broth, tomatoes, zucchini, salt, and pepper; bring to a boil. Reduce heat to medium-low, and simmer, stirring occasionally, 10 minutes. Stir in beans and pasta, and cook, stirring occasionally, 10 to 12 minutes or until pasta is tender. Top each serving with 1 to 2 basil pesto.

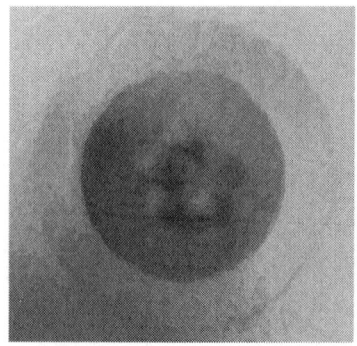

Caribbean Tomato & Peanut Soup

2 tablespoons vegetable oil
2 onions, minced
2 tablespoons all-purpose flour
3 cups milk
½ cup smooth peanut butter
1 teaspoon celery salt
3 cups tomato juice
Black pepper to taste

Heat oil in a large saucepan. Add onions and cook until soft but not brown. Add flour and stir 2 minutes over low heat. Remove saucepan from heat. In a medium bowl, stir milk slowly into peanut butter until mixture is smooth. Add celery salt and pepper. Stir milk mixture slowly into onion mixture. Return pan to medium heat and cook, stirring often, until liquid thickens. Do not boil. Stir in tomato juice and refrigerate at least 1 hour before serving. Makes 6 servings.

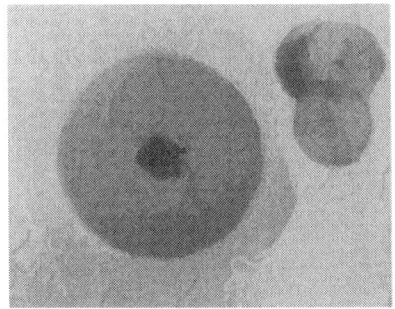

Caribbean Papaya & Garlic Soup

4 cups vegetable stock
3 cups chopped papaya pulp (3 to 4 papayas)
8 garlic cloves
½ pint (1cup) whipped cream
Salt and freshly ground black pepper

In a large pot, mix stock, papaya and garlic. Bring to a boil. Reduce heat and simmer 45 minutes. Add cream and heat through, then season to taste with salt and pepper. Puree in a blender or food processor fitted with the steel blade. Return soup to pan and reheat. If it seems too thick, add more stock. Serve immediately. Makes 6 servings.

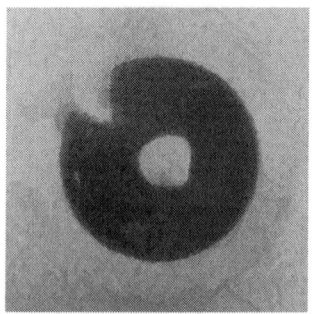

Cuban Vegetarian Black Bean Soup

½ pound dried black beans
4 cups water
4 cups of vegetable stock
¼ cup dry sherry
Salt and freshly ground black pepper to taste
3 cups hot cooked rice
½ cup chopped green onions
1 small onion, finally diced
1 small jalapeno pepper, diced
2 garlic cloves
¾ tsp. salt
¼ tsp. black pepper

Rinse and sort beans. Place in a medium bowl and cover with several inches of cold water. Soak overnight. Drain beans; place them in a large pot. Add the 4 cups water and stock, then simmer 2 hours, or until beans are tender. Heat vegetable oil in a pan. Add diced jalapeno pepper to hot oil until they begin to brown. Add diced onion and garlic to the hot oil. Cook until the onions are soft. In a blender or food processor fitted with steel blade, puree half of the beans. Return pureed beans to pot along with sherry and the diced onion, garlic and jalapeno oil mix. Reheat gently and season to taste with salt and pepper. Serve with rice. Pass green onions separately. Makes 6 servings.

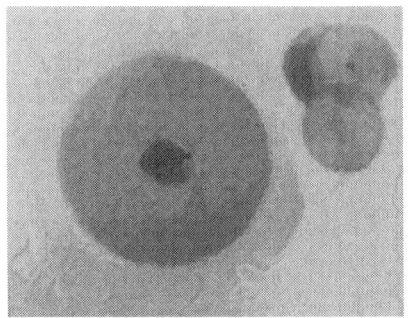

Bean Soup

16 oz. white kidney beans, rinsed, drained and cooked
1 medium onion, chopped
1 medium carrot, sliced
1½ cup vegetable stock
¼ cup white wine (optional)
¼ teaspoon dried leaf tarragon
½ cup water
1 teaspoon low-sodium soy sauce
Juice from ½ lemon
1-1/2 cups shredded romaine, escarole or spinach
2 or 3 tablespoons minced pimento

Sauté onion and carrot in ¼ cup stock and wine, if desired, till soft. Add tarragon. Add onion mixture, beans and remaining stock to a food processor fitted with the metal blade; puree till creamy and smooth. Pour into large saucepan, add water and soy sauce and heat thoroughly. Remove from heat. Add lemon juice, romaine and pimento. Stir to wilt romaine. Serve hot. Makes 6 servings.

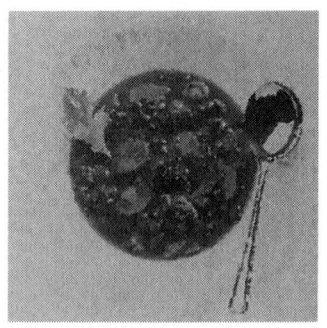

Lentil Soup

2 cups lentils, rinsed
6 medium onions, sliced
6 cups of water
3 cups of vegetable stock
¾ cup chopped onion
¾ cup chopped celery
½ cup chopped carrots
½ cup chopped leeks
6 large Baby Bella mushrooms, sliced
1 clove garlic, minced
1 small jalapeno pepper
1 bay leaf
½ teaspoon thyme
2 teaspoons salt
¼ teaspoon pepper
2 tablespoons vinegar

Combine lentils with water and vegetable stock in large kettle. Bring to boil, reduce heat, and simmer 35 minutes, stirring occasionally. Finally chop the jalapeno pepper and sauté in skillet of hot oil. Before the peppers change colors add sliced mushroom for a light fry. Add onion, celery, carrots, leeks garlic, bay leaf, thyme, salt, and pepper. Cook and stir for 4 minutes. Add this to lentils and simmer 25 minutes longer, stirring occasionally. Add vinegar. Bring to simmer and remove from heat. 6 to 8 servings.

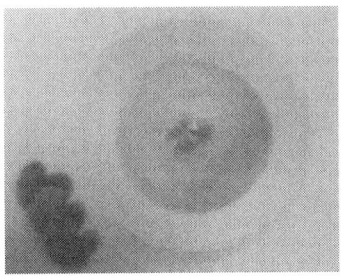

Green Summer Soup

6 cups vegetable stock
1½ cup of chopped spinach
2 cups mixed greens: salad burnet, outer leaves of lettuce, borage leaves, comfrey leaves
½ cup chopped green onions
1-1/2 teaspoon chopped tarragon
1 cup chopped celery
1 cup finely grated carrots and a few chopped carrot tops (¼ cup)
¼ cup chopped parsley
1 teaspoon butter
2 teaspoon flour
Salt and black pepper to taste
½ cup fresh yogurt

Sauté the chopped onions, celery and carrots in the butter. Add the stock, salt and pepper, spinach, and the mixed greens. Simmer for 10-15 minutes. Liquidize. Take ½ cup of the soup and stir in the flour. Return the soup to the pot, add the flour mixture and stir until thickened. Stir in yogurt. Serve either hot or cold with a sprinkling of chives and tarragon.

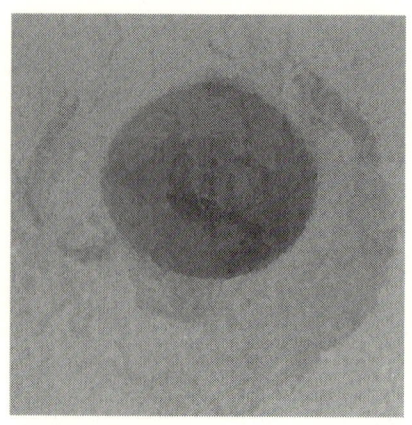

Carrot Cream Soup

1 pound carrots, chopped
1 onion, chopped
2 tablespoons oil
6 cups of water
½ teaspoon salt
⅓ cup parsley, chopped finely

Sauté the chopped onions and carrots in the oil for 5 minutes in a large pot. Add water, parsley and salt. Bring to a boil. Reduce heat, cover, and simmer for 20 more minutes. Puree mixture and reheat.

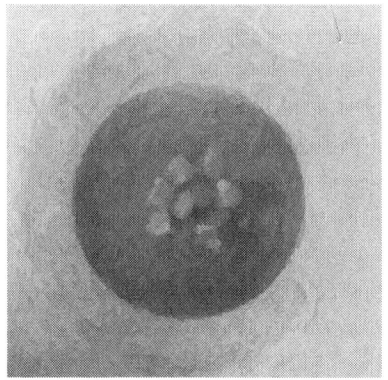

Avocado & Ginger Vichyssoise

½ cup of butter or margarine
1 medium onion, finely chopped
1 teaspoon ground ginger
1 large avocado, mashed
2 cups vegetable stock
1 teaspoon salt
½ cup half and half
1 green onion, finely chopped

Melt butter in a large saucepan over medium heat. Add onion. Cook until softened. Add ginger and cook, stirring, 2 minutes. Add avocado and stock, mixing with a whisk to avoid lumps. Simmer slowly 10 to 15 minutes, then add salt and half and half. Stir thoroughly, then cool slightly. Cover and refrigerate soup at least 1 hour. Garnish each serving with chopped green onion. Makes 6 servings.

Veggie Chili

2 large zucchini, chopped
1 large yellow squash, chopped
1 large onion, chopped
2 tbsp. olive oil
½ tsp. table salt
1 (12-oz.) texturized vegetable protein
1 8oz. cooked red beans
1 package of chili starter seasoning

Sauté zucchini, squash, and onion in hot oil in a large Dutch oven over medium-high heat 3 to 4 minutes or until tender. Add salt and meatless ground crumbles, cook one minute. Stir in chili starter seasoning. Bring to a boil over medium-high heat; reduce heat to medium-low, and simmer, stirring occasionally, 10 minutes. Makes 6 cups.

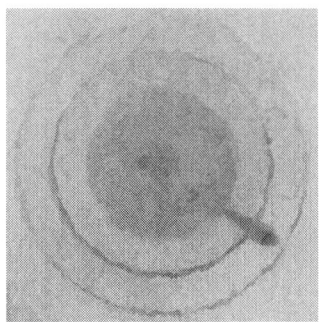

Lima Bean Soup

2 cups of cooked lima beans
2 cups of tomato juice
1 cup of water
6 spinach leaves
10 sprigs of parsley
½ tsp. of salt
½ tsp. of black pepper

Add cooked lima beans to tomato juice and water, boiling for 15 minutes. Add cooked spinach and fresh parsley to the boil. Add salt and pepper to taste. Simmer heat to low temperature for 15 minutes more or until beans are fully cooked.

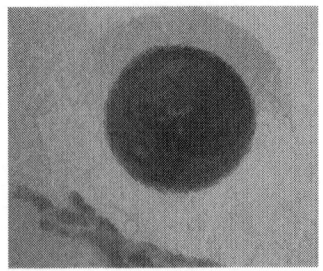

Hawaiian Red Bean Soup

2 cups of red beans
1 small onion, sliced
1 clove garlic, cut fine
1 large potato
1 small cabbage
½ cup macaroni
1 tablespoon of oil
1 can tomato sauce
2 quarts of water
2 tablespoons lemon juice
Paprika and cayenne
½ tsp. salt
½ tsp. of black pepper

Cook beans in plenty of water until tender. Add onion, garlic, diced potatoes, salt, pepper, oil and cook 15 minutes. Add tomato sauce and cook 5 minutes more. Add the water and lemon juice. Mix and boil until vegetables are well done. Add cabbage and macaroni and cook 15 minutes more.

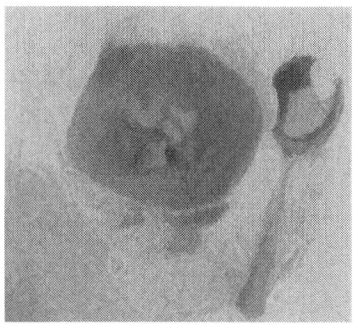

Sweet Potato Soup

2 tbsp. buttermilk
1 medium onion, chopped
2 garlic cloves, minced
5½ cups vegetable broth
2 lb. sweet potatoes, peeled and chopped (2 large)
1 cup apple cider
1 tsp. minced canned chipotle pepper in adobo sauce
1 tsp. table salt
2 tbsp. fresh lime juice
½ cup sour cream
2 tsp. fresh lime juice
Smoked paprika garnish

Melt butter in a large saucepan over medium-high heat; add onion, and sauté 5 to 7 minutes or until tender. Add garlic, sauté 1 minute. Stir in broth, sweet potatoes, apple cider, chipotle pepper in adobo sauce and salt. Bring to a boil. Reduce heat to medium-low, and simmer 20 minutes or until potatoes are tender. Process mixture in blender until smooth. Return to saucepan. Cook potato mixture over low heat, stirring occasionally, 5 minutes or until thoroughly heated. Stir in 2 tbsp. lime juice. Ladle soup into bowls and drizzle each serving with sour cream mixture. Garnish with fresh cilantro springs, smoked paprika.

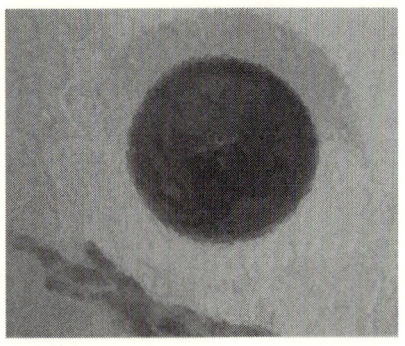

Chilled Beetroot Soup

3 beetroots (large)
6 cups of herb or vegetable stock
1 cup of yogurt
½ cup sour cream
½ cup chopped celery
½ cup chopped dill
Juice of 1-2 lemon
Salt and pepper to taste

Grate beetroots and boil up in vegetable or herb stock for 10 minutes. Set aside to cool, then put through a liquidizer. In a bowl blend yogurt, sour cream, chopped herbs, salt and pepper. Chill. Just before serving blend in the liquidized beet-root and stock, lemon juice and yogurt and herb mixture. Serve chilled with a sprinkling of chopped dill. Serves 5.

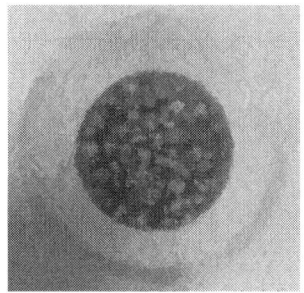

Fresh Summer Salad in a Soup

8 to 10 large heirloom tomatoes cut into 8 wedges each
2 medium tomatoes
2 tbsp. extra virgin olive oil, divided
¾ tsp. sea salt, divided
¼ tsp. sugar
2 small yellow squash, thinly sliced
½ English cucumber, diced
½ cantaloupe, cut into 1/2-inch pieces
1 pt. assorted small tomatoes, halved
1 cup blueberries, halved
1 tsp. fresh thyme leaves

Process heirloom tomatoes in a food processor 30 to 60 seconds or until pureed. Line a colander with 2 layers of cheesecloth; place colander over a large bowl. Pour tomato puree into cheesecloth. Tie ends of cheesecloth together. Chill 24 hours to allow puree to drain. Remove bowl from refrigerator, and gently press cheesecloth using back of a spoon to extract remaining liquid. Yield should be about 4 cups. Cover and chill. Preheat oven to 250 degrees. Core medium tomatoes, removing stem ends. Cut tomatoes in half; place, cut sides up, on a lightly greased aluminum foil-lined baking sheet; sprinkle with 1 tbsp. olive oil, ¼ tsp. sea salt, and ¼ tsp. sugar. Bake 2 hours. Place I roasted tomato half in each of 4 serving bowls. Top with squash and next 4 ingredients; sprinkle with thyme and ¼ tsp. salt. Add remaining ¼ tsp. salt to tomato water, and divide tomato water among bowls. Drizzle olive oil, and serve immediately.

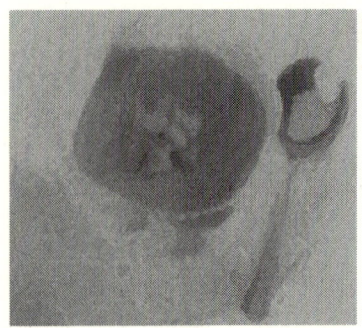

Perky Squash Soup

1 medium onion, coarsely chopped
1 clove garlic, crushed
2 tbsp. butter or margarine, melted
4 medium size yellow squash, sliced ¼ inch thick
1 cup of vegetable broth
1 8oz. can of tomato sauce
1 ½ cup water
½ tsp. salt
½ tsp. freshly ground pepper
½ tsp. parsley flakes
¼ tsp. dried whole thyme
1/8 tsp. dried whole oregano
Grated Parmesan cheese

Sauté onion and garlic in butter in a Dutch oven until tender. Add remaining ingredients, except cheese. Cover and simmer 20 minutes, or until squash is tender. Top with cheese. Yields six cups.

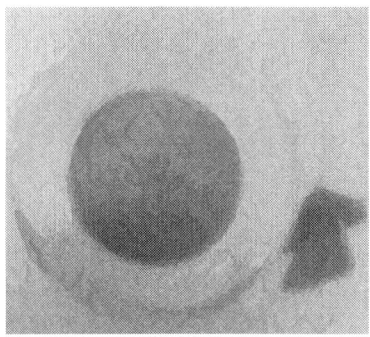

Collard Green Pistou

2 cups firmly packed chopped fresh collard greens
2 garlic cloves
2/3 cup extra virgin olive oil
¼ tsp. dried crushed red pepper
2 tsp. lemon zest
1 tbsp. fresh lemon juice
¾ tsp. table salt
¼ tsp. black pepper

A pistou is a cold hearty sauce that can be added directly to a bowl of your hot vegetable soups. For this pistou, boil your collard greens in boiling salted water for 4 to 6 minutes or until tender, drain. Plunge into ice water to stop the cooking process; drain well. Process garlic in a food processor until finely ground. Add greens, olive oil, and red pepper. Process 2 to 3 seconds until finely chopped. Stir in remaining ingredients.

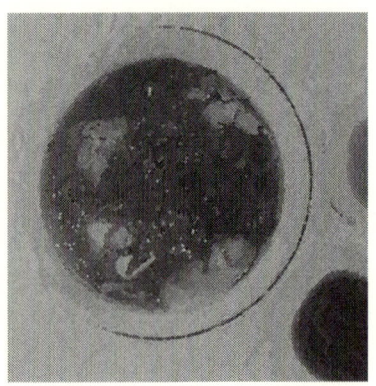

Turnip Green Soup

2 large onions, chopped
2 cans navy beans, drained and rinsed
1 tbsp. sugar
2 packages of frozen turnips with roots
½ cup of vegetable oil
2 large potatoes, diced
2½ cups of water
1 small onion, diced
1 small jalapeno pepper, seeds removed, diced
2 garlic cloves
¾ tsp. salt
¼ tsp. black pepper

Heat vegetable oil in your boiling kettle. Add diced jalapeno pepper to hot oil until they begin to brown. Add diced onion and garlic to vegetable oil and jalapeno mix. Cook until the onions are soft. Add water and bring to a boil. Add diced potatoes and frozen turnips. Bring to a boil. Add drained navy beans, sugar, salt and black pepper. Add water if necessary. Bring to a boil and reduce heat to low for 30 minutes.

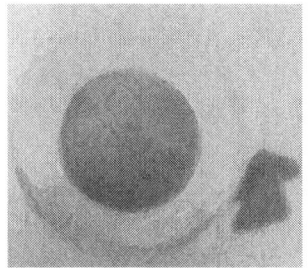

Cold Cucumber Soup

3 medium cucumbers
2 tablespoons butter
1 leek, chopped
2 bay leaves
1 tablespoon flour
3 cups of vegetable broth
1 teaspoon salt
1 cup half and half
Juice of ½ lemon
Chopped dill
Sour cream

Peel and thinly slice 2 cucumbers. Melt butter, add sliced cucumbers, leeks and bay leaves, and cook slowly until tender but not brown. Discard bay leaves. Add flour and mix well. Add vegetable broth and salt and bring to boil, then reduce heat and simmer 20 to 30 minutes, stirring occasionally. Puree through a sieve or in blender container and chill soup in refrigerator several hours. Peel, halve, and remove seeds from remaining cucumber, then grate. Add to soup with half and half, lemon juice, and chopped dill to taste. Serve in cold soup cups and top each serving with a dollop of sour cream. Makes 6 servings.

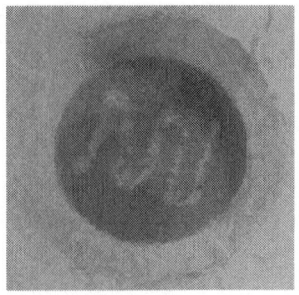

Smokey Red Pepper Soup

3 tbsp. butter
6 large red bell peppers, chopped
3 medium carrots, chopped
1 large sweet onion, diced
2 garlic cloves, minced
3 tbsp. tomato paste
1 tbsp. finely grated fresh ginger
2 tsp. smoked paprika
1 tsp. ground coriander
5 cups vegetable broth
2 bay leaves
¼ cup whipped cream

Melt butter in a large Dutch oven over medium-high heat; add bell peppers, carrots and onion. Sauté 12 to 15 minutes or until onions is golden. Stir in garlic, tomato paste, ginger, paprika and coriander. Cook, stirring constantly, 2 minutes. Add broth and bay leaves; bring to a boil over medium-high heat. Reduce heat to medium-low, and simmer, stirring often, 25 minutes or until vegetables are tender. Discard bay leaves. Process soup with a blender until smooth. Stir in cream, and season with table salt and black pepper to taste. Cook over medium heat 10 minutes or until thoroughly heated. Served with Collard Green Pistou (page 30).

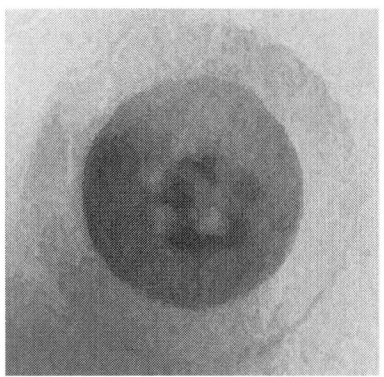

Creamy Tofu Tomato Soup

1 onion, diced
1 garlic clove, crushed
1 cup skim milk
Dash of Tabasco sauce
3 tomatoes, diced
12 oz. tofu
2 tablespoons minced parsley

Sauté onion and garlic over medium heat for 3 or 4 minutes in heated oil, until soft. Add milk, tabasco sauce and tomatoes, stirring constantly. Cool for 10 minutes. Pour into a food processor fitted with the metal blade. Add 10 ounces of the tofu. Process until smooth. Serve hot or cold. Cut remaining tofu into small cubes. Sprinkle with parsley and tofu cubes. Makes 2 servings.

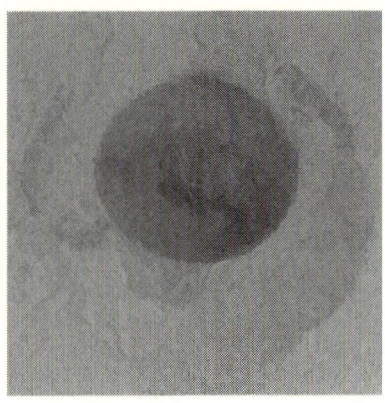

Onion Soup

2 large onions, thinly sliced
4 cups vegetable stock
2 teaspoons low-sodium soy sauce, or tamari
2 tablespoons dry sherry
Pepper to taste
2 teaspoons dried onion flakes
1-1/2 tablespoons onion powder

Sauté onions in a medium-size saucepan in a small amount of broth and soy sauce until translucent, about 10 minutes. Add remaining ingredients. Cover and simmer 20 minutes. Makes 4 servings.

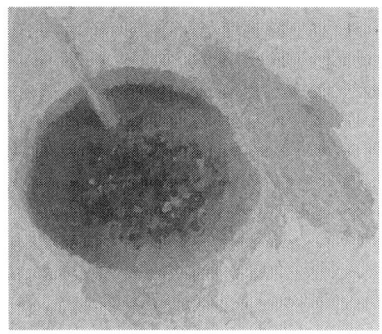

Cabbage Soup

4 cups vegetable stock
1 (8-oz) can no salt added tomato sauce
2 cups water
2 carrots, sliced
2 celery stalks, sliced
½ head cabbage, shredded
1 leek, white part only, chopped
1 medium-size onion, chopped
2 turnips, sliced
1 garlic clove, minced
½ cup of cauliflowerets (bite size cauliflower pieces)
2 tablespoons chopped fresh dill
2 tablespoons low-sodium soy sauce

Combine everything except dill and soy sauce in a large saucepan. Cook 1 hours until vegetables are tender. Add dill and soy sauce. Cook 15 minutes. Serve hot.

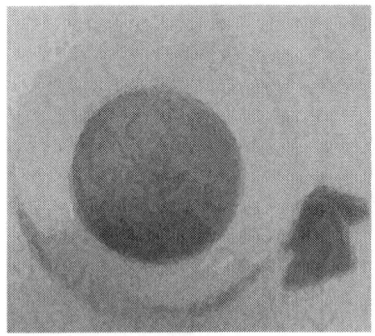

Cream of Broccoli Soup

1 pound broccoli, chopped
½ pound mushrooms, chopped
1 small onion, chopped
1 teaspoon tarragon
3 cups of milk

Steam vegetables and onion together for 10 minutes. Blend half of the steamed vegetables in a blender or food processor with 1 ½ cup of milk. Pour into a pot. Blend remaining vegetables and milk. Add to pot. Season and reheat for 5 minutes over medium heat. Add water if thinner soup is desired. Serves 8.

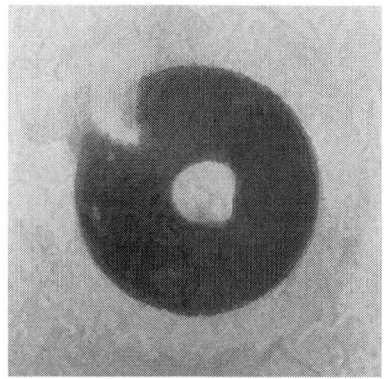

Hot and Sour Soup

8 cups vegetable stock
½ head napa (Chinese) cabbage, cut into medium dice
5 oz. shiitake mushrooms, stemmed and sliced
3 medium carrots, peeled and cut into julienne strips
5 oz. of sliced bamboo shoots, cut into julienne strips
3 tablespoons low-sodium tamari soy sauce
2 teaspoons grated fresh ginger
8 oz. low-fat firm tofu, cut into small dice
2 tablespoons rice vinegar (brown or white)
1/8-1/4 teaspoon cayenne pepper
3 tablespoons cornstarch
3 tablespoons water
1 bunch green onions, thinly sliced

In a soup pot, combine stock, cabbage, mushrooms, carrots, bamboo shoots, soy sauce and ginger. Bring to a boil, reduce heat to low and add tofu. Simmer for 15 minutes. Stir in vinegar and cayenne to taste. In a small bowl, combine cornstarch and water to make a paste. Stir into soup. Heat soup gently until it thickens, about 5 minutes. Ladle soup into bowls and garnish with sliced green onions and wonton curls, if desired. 8 servings.

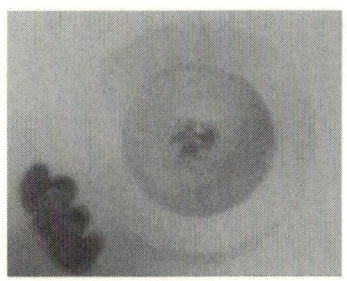

Indian Pea Soup

¾ pounds of peas
1 ½ oz. butter
1 teaspoon ground cumin
1 teaspoon ground coriander
½ teaspoon tumeric
¼ teaspoon fenugreek
½ teaspoon ginger
1 teaspoon poppy seeds
1 oz. raisins
1 teaspoon paprika
Small pinch cayenne
1 pint of vegetable stock
½ tablespoon flour
¼ pint top of milk
Salt to taste
1 teaspoon sugar
1 oz. split almonds

Cook the peas until very soft. Liquidize and put through a sieve. Melt ½ oz. of the butter in a large pan and add the spices. Cook over a low heat for several minutes. Add the puree and the stock and bring to simmering point. Melt the remaining butter in a small pan and stir in the flour to make a roux. Cook for a few minutes and stir in the milk. Stir into the pea puree, and keep hot but do not boil. Season with sugar and salt. Add the almonds and raisins.

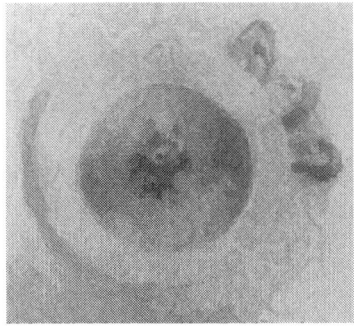

Potato and Leek Soup

3 leeks, halved lengthwise, washed thoroughly and sliced (4 cups)
1 large onion, chopped
4 large baking potatoes, peeled and cut into chunks
3 quarters vegetable stock
⅛ teaspoon of sea salt
¼ teaspoon freshly ground black pepper
2 tablespoons snipped fresh chives
Non-stick cooking spray

Spray a large soup pot once with cooking spray and set over low heat. Add leeks and onions, cover pot and cook for 10 minutes, stirring once or twice. Add potatoes and stock. Bring to a boil, then reduce heat to medium-low. Simmer until potatoes are soft, about 20 minutes. Puree soup in batches in a blender or food processor. Season with salt and pepper. Reheat gently and serve hot. Garnish with chives. 10 to 12 Servings.

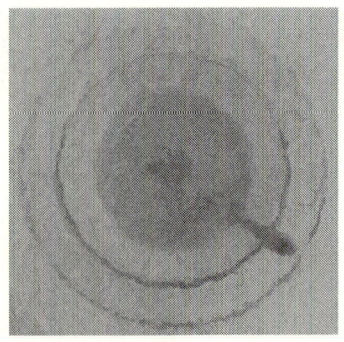

Zucchini and Potato Cream Soup

1 small onion, chopped
2 tablespoons oil
3 or 4 medium zucchini, chopped
2 potatoes, cubed in small pieces
6 cups of water
½ cup rolled oats
½ teaspoon salt
2 tablespoons parsley

Sauté onion in oil. Add chopped zucchini and cubed potatoes. Sauté for 5 minutes. Add water, rolled oats and seasoning. Simmer 15 minutes. Puree in blender, reheat, and serve. Serves 6.

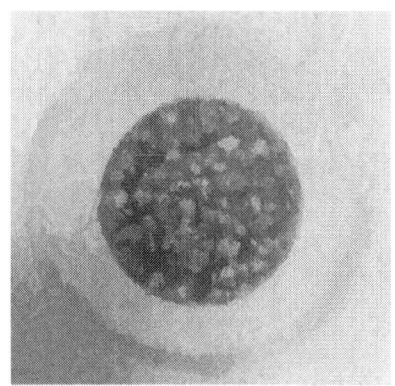

Vegetable Gumbo

1 small onion, diced
3 stalks celery, tough strings peeled, sliced
1 teaspoon chopped fresh garlic
1 14.5-ounce can diced low-sodium tomatoes with juices
4 cups fresh or frozen corn kernels
3 cups of sliced okra
2 medium boiling potatoes, peeled and cubed
7 cups vegetable stock
Sea salt and freshly ground black pepper to taste
Hot sauce to taste
Non-stick cooking spray

Spray a large soup pot with cooking spray. Heat pot over low heat. Add onions and celery, cover and cook for 2 minutes. Add garlic and cook for 15 seconds. Stir in tomatoes, corn, okra and potatoes. Add stock and bring to a boil. Reduce heat to a simmer. Cook until potatoes are soft and gumbo has thickened, about 30 minutes. Season to taste with salt, pepper and hot sauce. 12 servings.

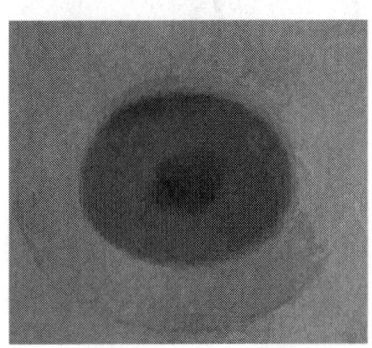

Chilled Fruit Soup

1 12 oz. can pitted bing cherries
6 oz. strawberries
4 oz. cantaloupe
4 oz. blueberries
4 oz. honeydew
2 tablespoons granulated sugar
1 teaspoons of cinnamon
¼ cup orange juice
1 tablespoon grenadine

Puree the cherries, strawberries, cantaloupe, honeydew and blueberries in a blender. Add sugar, grenadine, orange juice and cinnamon. Stir well to dissolve the sugar. Chill until ready to serve. Serve with a dollop of any fruit flavored fat-free yogurt and fresh mint as a garnishment. You can substitute any fruit depending on the season or personal taste.

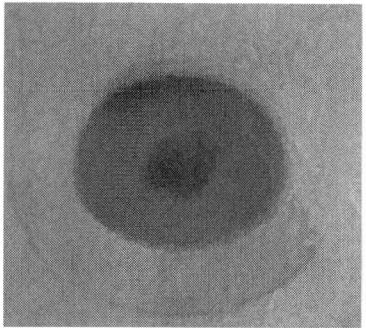

Minted Berry Soup

4 cups strawberries, boysenberries, or raspberries
¼ cup brown sugar, packed
¼ teaspoon salt
½ teaspoon cinnamon
¼ teaspoon cloves
1 (4/5-quart) bottle of sautérne
1 tablespoon chopped fresh mint or 1 teaspoon dried mint
1 envelope unflavored gelatin
1/3 cup cold water
Mint sprigs

Wash berries and, if necessary, hull. Crush berries lightly with a potato masher or fork. Place in saucepan and stir in brown sugar, salt, cinnamon, and cloves. Add sautérne and bring to boil. Add chopped mint and simmer 2 or 3 minutes. Meanwhile, soften gelatin in cold water. Stir in boiling soup until dissolved. Pour into shallow pan and chill until thickened, about 3 hours. Pile jellied soup into chilled cups. Garnish each serving with a sprig of mint. Makes 6 to 8 servings.

Made in the USA
Columbia, SC
07 December 2018